The Dog of Truth

by
Susan Gates

illustrated by
Bistra Masseva

OXFORD
UNIVERSITY PRESS
AUSTRALIA & NEW ZEALAND

OXFORD
UNIVERSITY PRESS

Oxford University Press is a department of the University of Oxford.
It furthers the University's objective of excellence in research, scholarship,
and education by publishing worldwide. Oxford is a registered trademark
of Oxford University Press in the UK and in certain other countries.

Published in Australia by
Oxford University Press
Level 8, 737 Bourke Street, Docklands, Victoria 3008, Australia

ISBN 9780190318116

Series Advisor: Nikki Gamble
Printed in Singapore by Markono Print Media Pte Ltd

🐾 Chapter 1

Cal and his mum were at the Dogs Home. They were choosing a new pet. Cal looked into a cage. All he saw was a big heap of hair, like a giant floor mop.

The heap of hair raised its head. It stared right at Cal, as if it was begging him:

"Choose me!"

"I want this dog!" said Cal.

"No, that dog's not right for us," said Mum.
"He's far too old."

"*Please*," begged Cal. "It's my birthday tomorrow.
He could be my present!"

"We've already got your present," said Mum.

She moved on to a cage of cute little puppies.

The old dog's eyes looked so sad. Cal felt
really sorry for him.

"What's his name?" Cal asked Mrs Dent,
who ran the Dogs Home.

"His name," she told Cal, "is the Dog of Truth."

Chapter 2

"That's a weird name," said Cal. "Why's he called that?"

"Because he has amazing powers," whispered Mrs Dent. "He knows when you're telling the truth."

"You're joking!" exclaimed Cal.

"Watch," said Mrs Dent, quietly.

She put her hand in the cage and said, "I had cornflakes for breakfast."

The Dog of Truth sniffed Mrs Dent's hand.
Suddenly, his long, droopy ears started whirling
around, like two helicopters.

"See?" said Mrs Dent. "That's what he does
when he sniffs a lie. I actually had toast and jam."

Now that Mrs Dent was telling the truth,
the dog's ears stopped twirling.

"*Wow!*" cried Cal.
"I'd love a dog like that."

"That's what everyone says," Mrs Dent told Cal.
"Lots of people take him home. But they always
bring him back."

"Well, I won't bring him back," said Cal. "I'm
going to keep him forever!"

And he went rushing off to persuade Mum.

From his cage, the Dog of Truth watched Cal with sad, wise eyes. He looked as if he was thinking:

**"You'll bring me back. Cal.
Just like all the rest."**

Chapter 3

Mum took a *lot* of persuading. But at last, she gave in. Now they were driving home with the Dog of Truth on the back seat.

Cal was really excited. *I'm not telling anyone about my new pet's amazing powers*, he thought. *It's going to be my big secret.*

Cal got out of the car with the Dog of Truth. Just then, his friend Emma walked past, eating some chocolate.

"Chocolate – my favourite!" exclaimed Cal. "Can I have some?"

"Sorry," mumbled Emma. "I've just eaten the last bit."

Sniff, sniff, went the Dog of Truth. Suddenly, his ears started twirling like bicycle wheels.

"I bet if you look, you'll find that's not true," said Cal, grinning.

"Oh – er, yes! I've just found some in my pocket," said Emma, giving a piece to Cal.

After Emma had gone, Cal told the Dog of Truth, "Now I'll know when my friends are telling fibs!"

It was going to be a lot of fun.

🐾 Chapter 4

"That dog really smells!"
said Mum, later that day.

So Cal put the Dog of Truth in the bath, with lots of soapy bubbles. Mum came in to help.

"Have you done your homework?" she asked Cal.

"Of course I have!" said Cal.

The Dog of Truth sniffed at Cal's arm. Straightaway, his ears started twirling. Big, glossy bubbles, with rainbows inside, floated all over the bathroom.

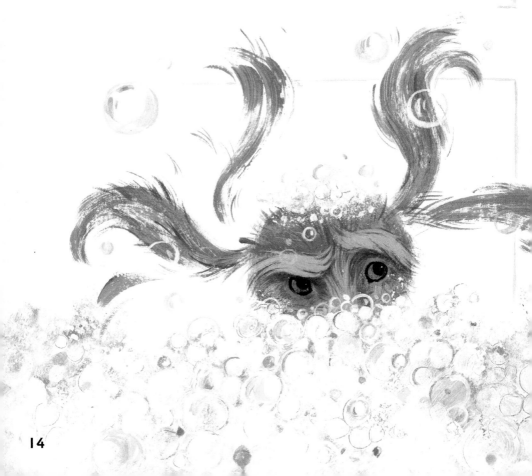

"What's the matter with him?" asked Mum.

"I don't know," said Cal, blushing bright red.

Now the Dog of Truth's ears twirled even faster!

"Hey, Dog of Truth!" Cal protested, when Mum had gone. "You're not supposed to twirl your ears at my lies!"

The Dog of Truth gazed at Cal with sad old eyes, as if to say:

"A lie is a lie, whoever tells it."

Cal muttered, "Maybe owning a Dog of Truth won't be as much fun as I thought!"

Chapter 5

The next day, Cal tore open his birthday present. He really wanted his own phone. But it wasn't a phone.

"It's a video camera," said Mum. "Do you like it?"

"It's a really cool present," said Cal, forcing a smile. "It's just what I wanted."

Instantly, the Dog of Truth's ears started twirling. Cal shot him a furious look.

"Why does he do that?" asked Mum.
"Does he know something we don't?"

Cal shoved the camera in his backpack.

"Come on!" he hissed at the Dog of Truth.

"Let's go to the park before you get me into trouble."

In the skate park, Cal saw his friends, Jack, Rahul and Emma. They were whizzing

up and down ramps,

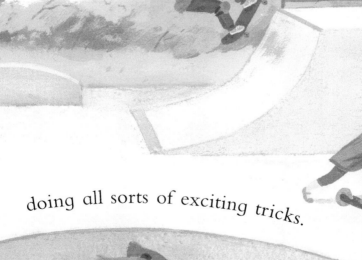

doing all sorts of exciting tricks.

Cal shouted, "Hi, guys! Are you practising for the competition? Why didn't you tell me? I thought I was in the team."

Rahul wouldn't look Cal in the eye.

"We tried to phone your house," he muttered. "But no one was home."

The Dog of Truth sniffed at Rahul's leg. Suddenly, his ears twirled like wind turbines.

"You *didn't* try to phone!" Cal accused them, angrily. "I *know* you didn't!"

All three of them looked very embarrassed.

At last, Jack stammered, "Look, um, I'm sorry,
Cal. We're still your friends. But the truth is, er,
you're no good at skateboarding. With you on our
team we'd never win."

Chapter 6

Cal watched his friends rolling
away on their skateboards.
He shouted, "I never liked
skateboarding anyway!"
But in his whole life, he'd
never felt so hurt
and lonely.

"This is all your fault," he told the Dog of Truth,
angrily. "You're just too much trouble. I'm taking
you back to the Dogs Home RIGHT NOW!"

The Dog of Truth gazed at Cal with his wise old eyes as if to say:

"Sometimes, Cal, the truth is hard to bear."

"I really wanted to be part of the team. But what can I do about it now?" groaned Cal, spreading his arms out hopelessly. "Nothing!"

The Dog of Truth's ears started
twirling like mad.

"Are you saying that isn't the truth?"
demanded Cal, puzzled.

Woof! Woof! barked the Dog of Truth.

"So what *can* I do then?" asked Cal. He had
no idea.

Could he get good at skateboarding? There
was no time — it was only two days until the
competition. Could he be the team mascot?
No, that would be silly.

Then suddenly he remembered his birthday present and he had the most brilliant brainwave.

He went racing back to
the skate park, with the Dog
of Truth trotting behind him.

"I'm going to make a video of
you guys with my new camera,"
he shouted. "So get ready! Do your
best skating ever!"

"That was *awesome!*" Cal said, when he'd finished his video. "I really enjoyed that!" And this time, the Dog of Truth's ears didn't move at all.

Cal's friends crowded around to see his video.
"Look at me doing that jump," said Rahul.
"I look like a skateboarding star!"
"I think that's my best kickflip ever!" said Emma.

"You're really good at filming," Jack told Cal.
"Will you make a video of us at the competition?"

"*Please!*" they all begged.

"Of course I will!" replied Cal proudly, with
a big beaming smile on his face.

Chapter 7

Cal left the park with the Dog of Truth. There was a confident new spring in his step. He felt like he was walking on clouds.

"Who cares if I'm no good at skateboarding?" Cal said, happily. "I've found out I'm great at making videos! And that's all because of you!"

Cal patted his pet's shaggy head.

"Thank you, Dog of Truth," he said.

Woof! Woof! went the Dog of Truth, as if to say:

"I'm sorry for what I said before," Cal apologised. "Don't worry. I'll never take you back to the Dogs Home, and that's the truth!"

Sniff, sniff, went the Dog of Truth. But his ears didn't even twitch. Instead, his tail wagged happily, like a flag, because at last he'd found a home.

"And I'm *never* going to tell another lie in my whole life!" Cal promised.

Cal and the Dog of Truth walked home together, with the Dog of Truth's ears twirling like windmills.